ORIGINAL SC

WITH

APPROPRIATE SENTIMENTS,

WRITTEN FOR THE

ORDER OF ODD FELLOWS,

BY A

MEMBER OF THE BUD OF FRIENDSHIP LODGE,

CALNE, WILTS.

—

Then let us pray, that come it may,
As come it will for a' that,
When sense and worth o'er a' the earth
Shall bear the gree and a' that,
For a' that and a' that,
It's coming yet for a' that,
When man and man the warld o'er
Shall brothers be and a' that.

BURNS.

—

CALNE:
E. BAILY, PRINTER.

To George Page, Esquire,

THE PRESIDENT, TREASURER, AND TRUSTEE,

OF THE

CALNE WIDOW AND ORPHANS' FUND SOCIETY,

AND AN

HONORARY MEMBER

OF THE

"BUD OF FRIENDSHIP LODGE,"

OF THE

INDEPENDENT ORDER OF ODD FELLOWS, M. U.

Sir and Brother,

In offering to my Lodge, and the Manchester Unity in general, this small collection of simple songs, I feel much pleasure in inscribing them to you, not only as a mark of my estimation of a highly respected friend, but as an acknowledgement of my admiration of those principles he first taught me to venerate. Could I here insert the numerous testimonies I have, of the zeal and ability with which you have advocated those principles, and the disinterested attachment you have ever manifested for the cause of Odd Fellowship, I would do so; but lest I should be deemed guilty of adulation by those who know you not, I will confine myself to the assertion, that the man who by precept and example points the path to happiness and prosperity, is in every way deserving the respect and gratitude of an enlightened community.

In days of turbulence and disaffection like these, when talent and mischief are leagued with cunning and craft, surely there is no slight meed of praise due to him who, in Friendship, Love, and TRUTH, would remove the pinching want and honest poverty, which the designing avail themselves of as an incentive to evil:—no right-thinking man will entertain a doubt about it; and therefore, to you Sir, as a firm supporter of our best institutions, and an Order that is as well known for its devoted loyalty as it is for its extent and charity, I dedicate my humble lays, as the best means of ensuring for them an indulgent reception, and the success of that cause for which they are expressly written.

I have the honor to be,
Sir and Brother,
Your's in the bonds of the Order, F. L. & T.
A MEMBER
Of the Bud of Friendship Lodge.
No. 3102.

CALNE, Wilts,
November 30th, 1843,

ORIGINAL SONGS.

No. 1.

BID the soldier don his helm,
And his sabre let him wield,
To guard his sovereign's realm,
Upon the tented field:
Let St. George's banner fly
Over wide and turbid seas,
To brave, as it has done for aye,
The battle and the breeze.

CHORUS.

But brothers, we will hand and heart unite in this our cause,
So shall we work our mutual good and gain the world's applause.

2

There are those who deem us odd,
And so we are in sooth,
We honor those who under God,
Defend his sacred truth:
We love our country's cause,
We succour those who need,
We keep the peace, obey the laws,
And thus we're *odd indeed.*

CHORUS—But brothers, we will, &c.

3

Then brothers fill it high,
Fill high the crystal bowl,
Let love and friendship light each eye,
And reason fire each soul :
Let those who know us not,
In every clime confess,
Odd Fellows are a glorious lot,
So here's to them success.

  Chorus—But brothers, we will, &c.

No. 2.

There's nought in every stage of life,
However long we languish,
But grief, and care, and toil, and strife,
To add to mental anguish ;
But yet, Odd Fellows, you'll find, as mellows
A life of such disorder,
There is a boon, will heal all soon,
In our united Order.

  Chorus—But yet, Odd Fellows, &c.

2

We see the hardy prostrate fall,
With all their cares around them,
And horrors, that would e'en appal
The stout, too soon surround them;
But here one brother assists another,
And all are kindly tended,
There are not hands in Europe's lands
Like ours, so soon extended.

    CHORUS—But here one brother, &c.

3

When factious knaves disturb the State,
And plot their schemes of treason,
The wisest way is to abate
Mistaken zeal with reason;
'Tis thus the Order throughout the border,
Was never known to falter,
When evil and designing men,
Have menaced throne or altar.

    CHORUS—'Tis thus the Order, &c.

4

Then if we help the needy poor,
And oft befriend the stranger,
The wealthy may feel doubly sure,
They need not deem it danger
To stand beside us, to aid and guide us,
And hold us an ensample,
For every upright honest man
To take for an example.

    CHORUS—To stand beside us, &c.

No. 3.

A bright brimming bumper come fill fill for me,
Let every one drink as a man,
For, upon my word brothers, I can't bear to see
A jingling and half empty can;
For now I shall give you the toast of my heart,
And mind that you each one accord her,
The pledge that I ask for the bonny sweet-heart,
And the wife of each man of our Order.

2

We drink to our Queen, whom God bless with long life,
And her sweet little cherubs of love,
Our Queen shews to every good Odd Fellow's wife
The duties she learns from above:
She honors her husband, the Prince of her soul,
And therefore, come brothers accord her,
The heartfelt good wishes you'll find in the bowl
That you drain to the Queen of our Order.

3

Then once more fill high, 'tis the last glass I claim,
For I am sure you will join me with glee,
There is not a worthier, nobler name,
Than that of Prince Albert the free;
He's a pattern for men of his high high estate,
And I wish that we had some recorder,
To enter Prince Albert, the good and the great,
As a brother of our Loyal Order.
      Loyal Order,
To enter Prince Albert, the good and the great,
A brother of our Loyal Order.

No. 4.

There are those who prize riches, and station, and wealth,
And some who e'en stoop to obtain them by stealth;
But for me, I hold something much dearer than all,
'Tis the Calne Bud of Friendship, whose sweets never pall,
   Whose sweets never pall,
   Whose sweets never pall,
'Tis the Calne Bud of Friendship, whose sweets never pall.

2

As the roses of Sharon, once beauteous in bloom,
Shed rich o'er the landscape their fragrant perfume,
May the young Bud of Friendship e're flourish like these,
And lend to old England as balmy a breeze,
  CHORUS—As balmy a breeze, &c.

3

And ye who attend it like husbandmen well,
Let it bloom on the down, let it flower in the dell,
Have a care that no chill blasts of malice prevail,
To check its young growth or its beauties assail,
  CHORUS—Or its beauties assail, &c.

4

And then when you're old, you will certainly see
Your Bud from a sprig, prove a fine hardy tree,
That shall spread o'er the gray locks that once gave it aid,
In winter its shelter, in summer its shade,
  CHORUS—In summer its shade, &c.

No. 5.

The tee-totaller tells us, a poor simple soul,
There's nothing but poison in each brimming bowl,
But the Odd Fellow's answer should always be such,
As would prove that the danger is taking too much.

2

If you look for example to history's page,
You'll find that the wisest were wont to assuage
Their thirst, or their anguish, with wine, ruby wine,
It's the choicest of liquids, indeed 'tis divine.

3

Then brothers, fill up to the brim every glass,
We'll drink to the wife and the kind-hearted lass,
That loves an Odd Fellow and values the man,
That acts as he ought, and can toss off his can.

4

But those who like better John Barleycorn's juice,
May drink without dreading the wise man's abuse;
As again in the face of the world we assert,
That the moderate use of strong ale cannot hurt.

5

And those who like better good spirits, may drink,
Without the dread fear of eternity's brink,
Provided they quaff them as Odd Fellows should,
And tope good old spirits to keep spirits good.

6

Then let the tee-totaller, poor simple soul,
Believe there is poison in each brimming bowl,
But as for good fellows, they laugh at such stuff,
They can drink and leave off when they've all had enough.

No. 6.

Brothers, let us all unite,
    Hand heart for weel and woe,
Can a nobler cause invite?
    Surely we may answer, no!
We in thousands, can agree,
To dwell in social mirth and glee,
And forward stand a unity.
    Hand heart for weel and woe.

2

Peers and princes dwell in state,
    Brothers, mark! 'tis well they should,
The higher you exalt the great,
    The more conspicuous is their good;
But we in humble freedom may,
Jog along life's beaten way,
Content and happier far than they.
    Hand heart for weel and woe.

3

Men who know us not may think,
    Ah! poor deluded elves,
All we have to do is drink,
    Or in lodge enjoy ourselves:
But why on folly thus enlarge;
Fenced with truth and reason's targe,
We defy so false a charge.
    Ah! poor deluded elves.

4

What we simply do is this,
    Hand heart for weel or woe,
Punish those who do amiss,
    Or point the path that they should go;
And when a good man sinks to sleep,
We dry the tears his mourners weep,
His widow and his babes we keep.
    Hand heart for weel and woe.

No. 7.

When the Eagles of Italy hovered o'er *Cherhill*,
And *Studley* could boast of a strong hold of Rome,
When the Raven of Denmark foreboded the peril,
Of Britons, who cherish'd *old Calne* as their home;
What was left then for England but rapine and plunder,
And where was the peace that men anxiously sought,
The foeman had ruthlessly riven asunder
The ties that the life-blood of britons had bought.

2

But see now the contrast, Rome shorn of her glory,
Succumbs to the Leopard* of Albion in fear,
And her sons have once told to proud Denmark a story,
They trembled midst blood and in thunder to hear:

---

*The Leopard was the supporter of the arms of king Henry the Eighth, who shook off Roman sway in Church and State.

For England has gloriously won the world's freedom,
She has dashed to the dust the vile chain of the slave,
And now she holds out to the nations that need 'em,
The rights and protection her forefathers gave.

3

But see from the midst of this bright flame of beauty,
A jet of transcendent refulgence appear,
That lights every warm hearted briton to duty
He knows to be honor, he feels to be dear;
That bright flame is friendship, the bond of Odd Fellows,
It unites them for ever in love and in truth,
And therefore, we need not the law to compel us,
To succour our aged, and foster our youth.

No. 8.

I've roamed e're now in Calstone dell,
Where many a limpid mountain stream
Leaps gladly from its rocky cell,
To catch the sun's refulgent beam;
And there I've roved beneath its shade,
With grief and worldly care opprest,
And thought each dashing wild cascade,
An emblem of my troubled breast.

2

And there I've felt how soon again,
'Twould be my hard relentless lot,
To launch upon life's turbid main,
And quit this sweet sequestered spot;

And there I've envied every rill,
Each bush, each tree, and moss-grown stone,
The simple cot and rustic mill,
And all within that dingle lone.

3

But I have seen there winning smiles
That beamed on me from happier eyes,
And learnt from their endearing wiles,
To prize more dear and lovely ties;
And now I feel the world is nought,
Nor e'en the sweets of Calstone grove,
Unless united with the thought
Of her, whom there I learnt to love.

No. 9.

When others round us can combine,
   To seek their mutual good,
The cause that should most brightly shine,
   Should be best understood.
      Then brothers, join in this our plan,
        And let our acts shew forth,
      The upright independent man
        We value for his worth.

2

Odd Fellows should be firm and true,
   For 'tis a noble cause
To spread the precepts that imbue
   A reverence for the laws.
      CHORUS—Then brothers, join, &c.

3

An order based on truth and love,
    Can surely only tend
To shew the world, and daily prove,
    That world it would befriend.
      CHORUS—So brothers, join, &c.

4

Then let the knave and scoffer smile,
    'Twill surely bring them ruth
If such can feel, if they revile
    Our Friendship, Love, and Truth.
      CHORUS—So brothers, join, &c.

No. 10.

When the heart with grief is riven,
    Where then the balm?
It so needs, when want hath driven
    Far, peace and calm;
What shall then stay woe's infection,
When the tear of strong affection
Tells the troubled soul's dejection,
    Where then the balm?

2

When the fond bereaved mother,
    Seeks then the balm,
Choking sighs her grief to smother,
    Where then the calm

She so needs for babes deserted?
In a world of good perverted,
Clasping them half broken hearted,
    Where then the balm?

3

'Tis in bonds like ours, my brothers,
    Such find the balm,
Orphans smile, and widow'd mothers
    Find peace and calm;
When by heartless friends neglected,
Left alone, they sink dejected,
'Tis by us they are protected,
    Here then's the balm.

No. 11.

Awake friends, awake, to the cause we revere,
To the spread of the precepts Odd Fellows hold dear,
As who can gainsay them, or dare to disown,
They guard not the altar, they prop not the throne.
Odd Fellows are loyal, Odd Fellows are true,
Odd Fellows are steady,
Firm, staunch, and ready,
As friends in distress, and prosperity too.

2

They heed not the taunts of the simple, who sneer
At the ties that unite them, as *mystic*, as *dear*,
For they feel that they're bound both in heart and in hand,
To strive for the good of their own father-land.
    CHORUS—Odd Fellows are loyal, &c.

3.

Then Englishmen join in our Order that vies
With others in deeds of the highest emprise,
And help us to shew to the civilized world,
That virtue is safe 'neath our banner unfurl'd.
Odd Fellows are loyal, Odd Fellows are true,
Odd Fellows are steady,
Firm, staunch, and ready,
To be friends in distress and prosperity too.

No. 12.

N. G. the bright smiles that are beaming around,
Are those of right hearty Odd Fellows,
And I'll venture to say, in the wide world around,
You cannot find men to excel us:
N. G., N. G. we are rich, we are loyal, and true,
The promoters of virtue and order,
And we trust in our V. G. and also in you,
To punish the slightest disorder.

2

The Mason may live if he likes on the square,
And the world it may revel in riot,
But the Odd Fellow's object and laudable care,
Is to set an example of quiet:
N. G., N. G. may the good, and the honest, and just,
Unite then, as friends to the Order,
And then we shall flourish and triumph, I trust,
Over mischief, and want, and disorder.

c

No. 13.

Full many a weary year had fled,
Of life's allotted span,
E're I had learnt what friends foretold
Would wait me as a man;
And long I laugh'd at worldly cares,
And smiled at fortune's frown,
Until I found misfortune's tares
Were thickly round me strown.

2

The dangers of the world I'd braved
Had trod far foreign strands,
And many a trusty friend I'd saved
From care, in other lands;
But it at last came home to me,
I saw them round me fall,
And then, alas! I learnt to see
That grief's the lot of all.

3

I look'd abroad on all mankind,
And mark'd with mental pain,
The vilest passions were combined,
To work a worthless gain;
While want and evil raged around,
It wrung me to the core,
To see, where plenteous gifts abound,
Men beg from door to door.

4

Then though I boast not power, nor fame,
Nor wealth, my heart to steel
Against my soul's indignant shame,
For those who will not feel;
I have a right and noble cause
To nerve my feeble might,
And here I vow I will not pause
Till I defend its right.

5

My cause can help the simple poor,
Can aid the honest man,
Can peace and comfort well secure,
When sickness lays him wan:
It dries the tears of widow'd grief,
And kindly leads the young
To lisp their innocent belief
In God, with artless tongue.

6

Then let me call on good and great,
The rich, the priest, the peer,
To lend the might of high estate
To prop a cause so dear;
And if I'm asked to point the way
That leads to such an end,
ODD FELLOWSHIP, I boldly say,
To all that's good will tend.

No. 14.

That tolling bell, that tolling bell,
Is pealing out some dead man's knell,
And whilst its solemn sound I hear,
It seems to shake my soul with fear.

2

Fear! what have I to fear below,
That I should dread that sound of woe,
My path is open, and the smile
Of all I love, can care beguile.

3

For should it be ordain'd my doom
To sink into an early tomb,
There is a rock on which I trust,
The bonds of death and hell can burst.

4

And if for her who reigns supreme,
The fairy of my young love's dream,
I have a care—*my Lodge's arm*
Has strength to guard my own from harm.

5

And thus I feel supremely blest,
'Tis thus I lull my cares to rest,
And find *Odd Fellowship* imparts
A soothing balm to anxious hearts.

No. 15.

When death hath laid a friend or brother
On that dark cold bier,
Where widow'd wives and many a mother,
Drop the bitter tear;
Then in silent grief and sorrow,
We bear him to his tomb,
Thinking ours may be to-morrow,
Such another doom.

2

And if to-morrow's sun should find us,
Wrapt in that long sleep,
Leaving all our friends behind us,
O'er our graves to weep,
Wo'n't it be a sweet reflection,
As we close our eyes,
To have the Order's kind protection,
For our dearest ties?

3

Come, while life and health avail us,
Let us now invite
Men of every creed to hail us,
As the friends of right;
Then when Death, the ruthless tyrant,
Claims us as his own,
The grave, to some so dread and silent,
We shall deem a home.

No. 16.

On the opening of a New Lodge.

An Odd Fellow's temple this day is erected,
And its altar we've raised on Love, Friendship, and Truth,
For within its dear precincts the sad and dejected,
Must unite in the smiles and the pleasures of youth.

2

We know nought of discord, we suffer not malice
To darken the door of Odd Fellowship's fane,
But we fill for each friend from its bright brimming chalice,
The cup of affection we press him to drain.

3

O 'tis sweet to the soul to mark unity beaming
In eyes that are tell-tales of happiness too,
And to see the bright tear-drop of gratitude gleaming
In brilliancy, rivaling sunny May's dew.

4

Then, O! may this temple, this lodge of our Order,
Whose symbols are holy, whose emblems are peace,
E're take for its idol, its guide, and its warder,
That God, whose protection of right cannot cease.

No. 17.

O! could I but see that the great would not scorn
The pleasures and virtues that poor men adorn,
How soon would they shake the dark scales from their eyes,
And learn the poor man and his virtues to prize.

2

For wealth is a bauble, and greatness a bubble,
Attended with discord, dissention, and trouble,
But want with the poor man, tho' sad, and distressing,
Leads often to peace, and contentment, and blessing.

3

Men ask not for alms when their labor is wealth,
They seek not for help with employment and health,
But when sickness deprives them of both, then a friend
They look for for those whom they cannot defend.

4

Then ye who are noble and great in the land,
Stretch out in their need the Samaritan's hand,
And lend them your influence, give them your gold,
Their best and their dearest from want to uphold.

5

For see the bright star that has risen on high,
And shines in the zenith of every man's sky,
To lighten his path thro' this valley of tears,
And chase from his bosom a cruel world's fears.

6

That star is Odd Fellowship, glorious and great,
Like a key-stone securing the arch of the State,
Or a pillar erected to Friendship and Love,
Whose foundations malevolence never shall move.

7

Then hasten to hail it ye great, rich, and poor,
It will hurl desolation away from each door,
And give to the honest, the sober, and true,
The respect and esteem that to virtue is due.

No. 18.

There's glorious news in lodge to-night,
    So without further parley,
I'll sing with all my heart and might
    Hurrah for brother Charlie.
Its true he's tender, and *slim* and *slender*,
But I'll be bound to eat him,
If you don't find he's just and kind,
And worth a jovial greeting,

      Then come Odd Fellows, inflate your bellows,
      And sing both late and early,
      Here's health and wealth, success and pelf,
      To *leetle* brother Charlie.

2

'Tis true a Stewart held his crown,
    But like King James before him,
He from his throne at last came down,
    And Charlie walked up o'er him.
And now we'll toast him, and joke and roast him,
And I'll be bound to eat him,
If you don't find he's just and kind,
And worth a jovial greeting,

      Then come Odd Fellows, inflate your bellows,
      And sing both late and early,
      Here's health and wealth, success and pelf,
      And wha'll be host but Charlie.

No. 19.

On a brother mentioning he had seen a Butterfly on Friday, the 8th of December, 1843.

Hail, beauteous reveller in a summer's sun,
Is not thy race of life and flutter run?
How fleet thy glories, and how frail thy form,
To brave the blasts of chill December's storm.

2

This sunny day hath warm'd thy torpid chill,
To grace again the meadow and the hill,
And now thou sportest midst a winter's gloom,
As thou wert wont in summer's beauteous bloom.

3

Then if the kind and fost'ring hand of care,
Protects thy beauties, delicate as rare,
Sure in thyself a lesson I may learn,
Fraught with an interest to a world's concern.

4

'Tis this—that goodness, boundless as 'tis great,
Tempers the blast to each and every state,
And proves to man, that e'en an insect frail,
With Heaven's permission, braves a winter's gale.

5

Odd Fellows, brothers, let this insect teach
The certain truth of what God's servants preach,
That firm reliance on the Fount of Love,
Will fit a soul to flaunt in realms above.

D

THE AUTHOR'S FAREWELL TO HIS LODGE,

AN IMITATION OF

One of Lord Byron's Hebrew Melodies.

Farewell to ye, brothers, but e're I depart,
Accept at my hands the warm thanks of my heart,
And believe that your kindness, where e're I may roam,
Will lead me to look on my Lodge as my home.

2

For there I first vow'd to be loyal and true
To my God, and my queen, to my country, and you,
And as long as my heart in my bosom shall beat,
That vow I'll revere, and its promise repeat.

3

And then when I go to the wide world of men,
To buffet the tide of its surface again,
I shall look, as the tempest tost sailor distrest,
To the Calne Bud of Friendship, *my haven of rest.*

Bud of Friendship Lodge, Calne:
December 9, 1842.

SENTIMENTS.

1. *The Queen—the first in place, the first in power, and the first in the loyal Odd Fellows's affection.*
2. *The Pillars of the Order, and Bonds of the Unity.*
3. *The Bonds of the Order—may they be as soft as silk, but as strong as adamant.*
4. *May an Odd Fellow's Lodge be the Palace of Love, the Sanctuary of Truth, and the Temple of Friendship.*
5. *May Friendship triumph over Malice, Truth over Falsehood, and Love over Enmity and Evil.*
6. *May the principles of Odd Fellows be as well known as they should be as universally practised.*
7. *May Truth promote Unity, Unity foster Friendship, and Friendship ripen into Love.*
8. *May the order of this Order be so ordered, that the dis-order of the dis-orderly may never dis-order the order of this Order.*
9. *The Good Ship—Odd Fellow-ship; may she be steered with discretion, handled with skill, and defended with firmness.*
10. *The compass of Odd Fellow-ship, with the cardinal virtues for its cardinal points.*
11. *May the Buds of Friendship be the Flowers of Odd Fellowship.*
12. *Temperance, Sobriety, and Rectitude, the watchwords of the Order.*
13. *May Odd Fellowship be as preeminently distinguished for the oddity of its attachment to all that is high and noble, as it is now odd to find it united with evil and unworthiness.*

SENTIMENTS CONTINUED.

14. May all who, through ignorance of its principles, revile or despise Odd Fellowship, be speedily convinced of, and amend, their error.
15. May the life of every Odd Fellow be as smooth as glass, as clear as crystal, and as happy as the dove.
16. May Odd Fellows never forget their God, desert their country, forsake their neighbours, nor disgrace themselves.
17. May the success of Odd Fellowship astonish the world.
18. May Odd Fellows ever feel the holiness of their bonds, the sanctity of their ties, and the importance of their duties.
19. The way to be happy—The High Road of Odd Fellows, may it never be rendered rugged by the flinty hardness of stony hearts.
20. The Officers of our Lodge, and may the faithful discharge of their duties bring with it the reward so dear to every good man—an honest pride in well-done duty.
21. May we never cancel a PAGE from our Lodge Books.
22. May F. L. and T. be felt, learned, and taught.
23. May the suspended become high in the estimation of brothers.
24. The Board—may it never receive a French polish.
25. Open hands in open lodges.
26. May the pleasures of an Odd Fellow be his duties.
27. May every N. G. be v. g. and every V. G. N. G.

CONCLUSION.

MY work is done, I give the world my lays,
I dread not censure, and I ask not praise;
I am no hireling sycophant to fawn
Upon mankind, or feed on venom's spawn.
My book is written, and I only ask
The blessing of our God to rest upon my task;
Ye who would read it think when ye begin't
"A book's a book, although there's nothing in't;"
And if a moral you should find therein,
Pray let it plead for my presumptuous sin,
If you should deem it vanity to write
In the high cause of all that's good and right.
I am in heart and soul, first, I'll confess,
A staunch Odd Fellow, nothing more nor less;
And how that cause is graven on my heart,
Let my poor pen, and simple words impart
For it, in language of respect, I say
To those who claim it from their rank or sway;
I will be plain and honest—first, with you—
Giving to Cæsar always Cæsar's due,
Your's is a station raised by God, to show
That he o'er-rules the ways of all below;
Who props your glory, and who gives you health
To live in luxury, and roll in wealth?
My Order tells me God in heaven gave all,
The free his freedom, and the slave his thrall;
Then, noble Peers, I'd have it understood,
We know the value of right gentle blood,
We feel in you we have a guarantee
For all that's good, for all that's wise and free;
And that the mystic tie of gentle birth
Should be the guardian of all moral worth.

Priests. Priests of England, servants of the Lord,
Captains of Christ, who wield his two-edged sword,
Sons of the men who flew his flag unfurl'd,
High o'er the crescent and the pagan world;
You have a duty which we know is great,
But far removed from worldly pomp and state,
Known only well to wretched mourners' lot,
Done only well within the lowly cot—
Go seek such out, for such your master great,
Thought not too lowly for a God's estate;
And we have known a sainted * Bishop pray,
Beside a poor man on the hard worn clay.
Men. Men of Britain, who at ease repose,
Heeding alike the world and all its woes;
Think ye your duty you to God fulfill,
By shunning poverty and human ill,
No, I would tell ye that good gifts are given
For a wise purpose, by a bounteous Heaven;
And that for every talent ye possess,
Good must be done, be that good more or less.
And you, ye poor ones, who life's crooked way
Is plodded on with toil from day to day,
Who little know the griefs that riches shed,
And eat, in sweat, your hard earn'd daily bread;
You owe a duty to your God and man,

---

* The author has the following anecdote from a cottager, and will vouch for its truth. The late Honourable and Right Reverend Dr. RYDER, Bishop of LICHFIELD and COVENTRY, went one day into a cottage to pray with a poor man. But just as he was about to kneel on the hard brick floor, an inmate ran for a pillow, which he gently and mildly refused, with a remark that deserves a more conspicious place than this note. "Jesus Christ, my Master, never knelt upon a pillow, indeed he had not where to lay his head."

Which must be done, if you would shun the ban
That is entailed on broken laws and those
Who buy with sin on sin a hell's eternal woes.
If then my words are words of sober truth,
And we, in duty, must " give tooth for tooth,"
Let me ask all if they are acting well,
And let the answer each man's conscience tell;
And if 'tis duty to extend to all
A general good—then loudly let me call
On every man who has a heart to feel,
A lively interest in the public weal,
To aid our Order, and to test it well,
By every means the wise would seek to tell;
If it is based on what its precepts prove,
First, Friendship dear, and then, on Truth and Love:
Who can deny it? None, who know its ties,
Who can revile it? Surely not the wise;
Who can subvert it? None, it is too strong,
Already thousands to its cause belong;
And they will give with me this guarantee,
It is no paltry scheme of charity,
But a great means to save the human race
From many an evil that has stamped disgrace
On man, the lord of all the things of earth,
The noblest creature of creation's birth—
Then, those who find they feel they've grace, to own
They live not only for themselves alone,
Let them assume the dear and silken band,
That binds Odd Fellows both in heart and hand,
And show the nations of a mighty sphere,
They *live* and *love, protect, obey,* and *fear.*

INDEX.

Song, No. 1.   Air ..   *The Invincibles.*
   .. 2.   — ..   *Wha'll be king but Charlie.*
   .. 3.   — ..   *The king, God bless him.*
   .. 4.   — ..   *The Yorkshireman.*
   .. 5.   — ..   *The Roast Beef of Old England.*
   .. 6.   — ..   *Duncan Gray.*
   .. 7.   — ..   *Round Albion's loved shores.*
   .. 8.   — ..   *Ye Banks and Braes.*
   .. 9.   — ..   *Auld lang syne.*
   .. 10. — ..   *Poor Mary Ann.*
   .. 11. — ..   *Hearts of Oak.*
   .. 12. — ..   *Jolly Nose.*
   .. 13.
   .. 14. — ..   *Those Evening Bells.*
   .. 15. — ..   *Tom Bowline.*
   .. 16. — ..   *A Temple to friendship.*
   .. 17.
   .. 18. — ..   *Wha'll be king but Charlie.*
   .. 19.
   .. 20.

E. BAILY. PRINTER, CALNE.

Milton Keynes UK
Ingram Content Group UK Ltd.
UKHW020641120124
435917UK00007B/344